BACK ON THE BLOCK

BACK ON THE BLOCK

Written
By Ralph Watkins

First American Book

In Print

POETRY AND PROSE

Published 2016
Publisher: AUDAX, LLC.
All Copyrights Reserved copyright 2014
Email: dmvpoet@gmail.com
Published District Heights, M.D.
Print In America August 2021

Preface

First edition book of poetry written by Ralph Watkins Jr., designed for family, friends, and people of various cultures and mature age; that love reading modern, and urban literary creative work. Which embodies thoughts, feelings, and emotions. Often reflecting on life, family, and relationships experiences of a spiritual or secular nature, titled RAW Material in a text.

The body of work stretches over 40 years, from early childhood, youth, and military experiences, which encompasses and depicts various life, family, and some familiar experiences involving a relationship with other people. Poetry has always been a useful tool to share, encourage other people, and build bridges between two different places, to give people an easier and safer passage through words on a page.

One of my biggest dreams goes as far back as I can remember, and that is to be a creative writer of poetry and short stories. I did not take a direct path, and I was not always focused. But my heart was always in the right place. In my heart, I kept this love for writing poetry alive. Over the years I would revisit the thought of writing a complete book of poetry. I have arrived at a place in my heart, whereas I no longer want to put off my dream until tomorrow.

Contents

- R STREET — 8
- Nothing Like Yesterday — 9
- I Said Quietly — 10
- Don't Be A Punk — 11
- You Don't Want None — 12
- Don't Let People Get In Your Ear — 13
- I Didn't Do Anything — 14
- The Other Foot — 15
- For Those That Don't Know — 16
- I Am A One Winger — 17
- Not Funny — 18
- I Love The Attention — 19
- Ever Thought Back — 20
- I Was Born and Raised — 21
- It's A Thought Out Process — 22
- I Love You — 23
- I Grew Up Here — 24
- Heart It In Your Ear — 25
- I Love You — 26
- I Am Sitting — 27
- I Didn't Know — 28
- Exercise Daily — 29
- It's Sad To Think — 30
- Hush — 31
- It's Not What You Think — 32
- I Am Hope — 33
- I Opened My Eyes — 34
- Love Has A Way — 35

BACK ON THE BLOCK

- Part of Me — 36
- Through All These Years — 37
- I Grew Up In D.C. — 38
- Riding The Metro — 39
- No Day Was Every Promised — 40
- One of The Hardest Jobs — 41
- I Ain't Got to Tell You Nothing' — 42-43
- Don't Look At My Clothes — 44
- In The World — 45
- I Hit The Boiling Point — 46
- Sometimes While You Are Walking — 47
- I Shouldn't Tell You — 48
- I Need You — 49
- Those That Don't Me — 50
- I Remember — 51
- You Can't — 52
- I Just Want To Know — 53
- When I Dream In Color — 54
- In The Game of Chess — 55
- Even I Struggle Each Day — 56
- My Dad Was Always There — 57
- I Thought I Burned This Bridge — 58
- At The End of My Life Story — 59
- I Want To Go Straight — 60
- I Still Look Around For You — 61
- I Took You For Granted — 62
- We Thrive — 63
- Time Served — 64
- I Want You To Strong — 65

- Neighbor's Love R Street — 66
- Two Kinds of People — 67
- You Don't Know Your Child — 68
- People Can Be Mean — 69
- You're Not Alone — 70
- Civil Disobedience — 71
- You don't know shyt — 72
- Getting high — 73
- Real friends — 74
- LONG WAY FROM HOME — 75
- Keep Believing — 76
- 1st And R Street — 77
- AWAKEN — 78
- PHOTO SHOOT — 79
- IN YOUR EAR — 80-81
- In A Dark Place — 82-83
- Pick A Point — 84-85
- A Visit From Dad — 86-87
- Stung Twice — 88-89
- I Don't Have Time — 90-91
- My momma — 92-93
- When I Pray — 94
- What Are Brothers For? — 95
- Son — 96-97

NOTHING LIKE YESTERDAY

Nothing like yesterday. The flowers were in full bloom. I held you in my arms like I was never going to let you go, but that was yesterday don't know what has happened since then.

That season has passed, and the seed that was planted doesn't want to grow. I still look up at the sun, knowing that one day along with the rain, my chance at happiness will come again.

Tomorrow, I will look back but not forgetting where I came from. Here now, I wish all those that are waiting for their true love to arrive, just keep the faith and live anticipating the next raindrop. That comes along with the sun shining you will be dancing in the rain and start to grow.

I Said Quietly

I said quietly to the strange woman, as she took my money. "This is my first time." She mocked me by saying, "This is my first time, as well." As I pounced nervously up onto her layers of bed coverings. It was hard for me not to give thought to anything else. I said, "Be gentle and go slow. I want to etch this into my memory forever."

She laughed, and said, "By the end of the night, you won't remember a thing." We battled back and forth with the table lamp switch. I kept turning it on, and of course, she has wanted it off. Then, she said, "Dear boy, there's nothing for you to see." I struggled at first, to think about what I should do with my hands, and what words if any I should say.

She whispered in my ear, and I can't even repeat it; because it was in a language I didn't understand. I laughed and fell back. When I woke up in my bed the next day I realized I didn't lose anything, except maybe some sleep.

Don't Be A Punk

I don't want to be a punk

or someone walking around

holding their junk.

I like to be live and direct.

Treat people with respect.

I have also learned my place

on these streets called life.
I realize if I can not

give you the things you need;

 both time and love,

I don't want to park in that unoccupied
space in your life.

You Don't Want None

You don't want none of this.
Someone that is punch drunk.
Been hit so many times.
Don't know if I am laying down or still standing up.

When I hear the bell ring, win or lose I am throwing both my hands up. Life is too short to step outside of the ring, or call it quits.

When you lose your will to fight back or get up. That's when the next punch. That comes in, lands like a 747. Is felt and you know now looking up, that you have been hit.

Don't Let People Get In Your Ear

Don't let people get in your ear.
Don't let people get in get in your face.
People have a way of stepping on your toes.
Let them know that they are getting too close.

You have to have to have boundaries or people will walk all over top of you. Put up "No trespassing signs, 360 degrees, in plain view.

I am tired of sitting in silence, people always run away and take cover whenever my ignorance is displayed.

Don't ever let it get to that point. Just find a way to pardon yourself or just get up and walk away.

I Didn't Do Anything

I didn't do anything, well I did, but the crime does not fit the punishment. I was wrong based on a technicality. I was hungry, I went out for a walk and my travels took me into Mexico. I should have told you or anyone I was leaving out but I know, I made it pretty clear earlier that day, I was hungry.

What people fail to realize that you are part of my life, not all of life. And that's often where the missing understanding and broken marriages come in. I am not going to go biblical, because that's not where I am coming from.

If I were a pet you wouldn't be able to keep me tied up. So, what makes you think I am going to sit around and look stupid with my tongue hanging out? When I've made it perfectly clear with my hair falling out, that I am hungry.

Without further explanation, I believe in self-preservation, just don't go out there and make a fool of yourself, or embarrass anyone else in the process.

The Other Foot

This is about if the shoe was on the other foot. Imagine this, before it happens to you. No more flowers, candy, heartfelt words, or a lover's quarrel. Because they don't care anymore.

They don't even answer your phone calls or respond to your, "Let's try again to make it work text messages." This is when you start doing some soul searching, trying to figure out how to start over, or was I really that bad?

After being consoled by your mom, and your best friend, who's been warning you since the birth of the relationship, that person was never right for you, this just goes and proves it.

Shaking your head, not quite what you wanted to hear. But, I still love, and before you could finish your sentence, they encourage you to move on as best and as fast as you can.

I never really thought about how she felt. I knew she felt something, but I didn't know she would become completely numb. From her head to her toe, I can't even get her to turn her head to look at me. I tried calling her a thousand times.

FOR THOSE THAT DON'T KNOW

For those that don't know, ask somebody. The truth isn't always written on the wall. Mama' said, "You have to get in the house when the street lights come on!" Where are you now?

Did you fail to reach home in time, or you watched from a distance, the blinking of the porch light. I am sorry that you made a string of bad decisions, hopefully, when you get from behind bars, you will take advantage of the second chance.

I AM A ONE WINGER

I am a One-Winger, but I can fly and soar with the best of them. My secret is I believe in the one who created me, and I believe in myself.

I don't think His intentions were for me to fail, despite my physical appearance. It only appears to give me more of a challenge. I realize I have to reach the highest mountain with a plateau, so I can get a good running start.

But once I get out there, and get caught in an updraft, eagles bow at my presence, at the amazement of a bird with one wing.

Believing in themselves enough, and not accepting what you look like or what others may say to you. But everyone can fly, if you believe in yourself and really try.

NOT FUNNY

I don't even think it's funny, how other people's spirits won't you rest, and won't let us enjoy our time here on mother earth without jumping up and down, knocking things down, then vanishing, and disappearing. You have convinced me, we are not alone here. I don't like paying you any attention. My first instincts are to look and turn when I hear a thump or noise. you've had your time here and if you are not resting, you took a wrong turn.

Unfortunately for me, you're still unhappy and in 'get back mode'. Without me realizing it, I've allowed you to grow up with me, get inside my head, and help me make some pretty bad decisions over the course of my life. And, no I still don't want to talk to you aloud, because I don't want anyone to think I am going crazy, but a fool, I know you are there.

I know how to get rid of you, you, you, and you. My goodness, they are everywhere. I pray you away; I rebuke you in Jesus' name. I don't sit and play chess games, waiting for you to make your next move. I believe you have no place here and your only intentions are to destroy the lives of others.

 Our children are doing things they have no business, and it wasn't the way they were taught; marriages being severed in half, after vowing to be together for a lifetime. And people are having disagreements with each other worlds apart, and they don't even know why. I pray that you pray, not for just one or two, but for them all, to go away. Pray God gives you strength and peace, and He restores the love that was lost in your home. I know everyone is not going to agree with me, but we all agree that we are not acting alone, yet with some very disturbing and disruptive company, called spirits.

BACK ON THE BLOCK

I LOVE THE ATTENTION

I love attention, but its all the wrong attention that my family, friends, and coworkers give me. I hate the honey-do list, and the things the children give me. Work is an extended room outside of your house, that begs for the attention, that they are not getting at home, or growing up as a child.

I love the kind of attention when all the focus is on me, and since I am not modest, and I am in the center of the room on stage. At home, I am sitting or standing, something preferred when telling my family, and dog about my day at work.

All the integral details, but mostly the way I handle things, it really wasn't that hard. With friends, I just want to pause for a moment while you compliment me on my hair, shoes, or outfit. Just don't look and then look away without saying a thing. And for many, our safe haven and final resting place.

This kind of attention is confusing, way too much time is spent separating two people; or spending time in the corner yourself and defusing. I want peace at work, and for them to look at me like I was Gandhi. And walk around me, like I meditating for world peace. That's the kind of attention I want.

EVER THOUGHT BACK

Have you ever thought back, not taking away from what you have accomplished, to that child that you think is God gift to the world? Because if you haven't, look or think of the way, I assure you no one else will.

Moving right along, imagine if you just closed your eyes and let the boat that's anchored right there beside you or in some distant port, but you still have ties no matter where they are.

So now find ourselves preaching to our children when we didn't listen or follow instructions ourselves. We always wait in hope that the next generation does better or gets it right. We can't fault them when they're looking at us for setting a bad example.

I have looked back, and since, I can not go back and grammatically make any changes. I am at a place in my life where I ask God on a daily bases since I did not become an astronaut, help me deal with life on earth as best as I can, without me feeling like I could be living among the stars.

BACK ON THE BLOCK

I WAS BORN AND RAISED

I was born and raised Roman Catholic. We grew up playing in the streets dodging between parked cars, catching the football in moving traffic.

Our parents preached to us stay close to home and stick together when you walk to store, school, church, and grandma's house. And for us, life was never tragic.

We are a large family that lived in a small house, didn't all have the best of things, never went without anything and my parents always found a way to make it work or happen like magic.

Now, I am grown and have my own and they come with a price tag and everything they want or need I can't find or get at a bargain.

I try to like my parents to find a way to raise them to know God and enjoy life and look after one another. Most importantly take the positives out of growing up, so you can make the best of what you have. And pass that along without being a pain in society's butt or wreaking havoc.

IT'S A THOUGHT OUT PROCESS

It's a thought out process, and it consist of a meticulous planning. There were many nights I sat up crying and wondering if I got any of this thing right. I was overjoyed when you came into this world, and I was tickled pink when you took your first baby steps.

There were times when you got into stuff that you had no business and made a mess of everything. I didn't want to spank your little hands or legs, but I did, and I made you knew, that this was going to hurt me, more than it was going to hurt you. I think I started crying before you did.

Today, I smiled and cried as I watched my little girl look at me, and say, daddy, it's good seeing you as an adult. All I could think about, as I saw her first come into this world, almost twenty years ago.

I Love You

I love you, sounds like I have Gerber Baby
Food in my mouth; it just never sounds
right, so let me say it a different way.
I have known you like forever, and never
have I imagined life without you.

They say stars are countless in the heaven,
so they haven't realized they are missing
one I have always had what most people go
out and journey for I went out on that
same journey only to have it lead me back
to my front door.

I love you with the feeling of Gerber Baby
Food in my mouth because I have been
such a fool not to realize, I left my keys at
home.

I GREW UP HERE

I grew up here, 1st and R don't confuse me with the guys on T street, Lincoln Rd., or Q street close, but I am not one of them. Our block is longer, the guys are stronger, those we may not be related, stick together sisters and brothers.

I have been in their houses, ate their dinner table, and our moms and pops know each other. Its understood, don't let anybody bother you around here or even if you get out of the area.

Let someone know, and we all will take care of it. I always felt safe there. I did get my fair share of bruises. I think everyone goes some kind of rite of passage or pecking order, to see who the bad kids were. I just wanted to be accepted by my own, even if I had to punk someone myself.

Everything I learned while growing up, continue to play a part in my living today. Every now and then, someone tries to play you, and they may be in a group with three or four other guys. I am thinking this not going to be a good day for everyone. I grew up on 1st and R, and we roll just a little differently around here.

BACK ON THE BLOCK

Heard It In Your Ear

I know you heard it in your ear, "Stay out off them street" they will, if you not careful mess you up for life. They come at a price tag that neither one of us can afford, my children. If we are all sitting around about to sit down for dinner, or watching a little TV, and when it suddenly discovered that one of us is missing.

A shout out are given in the house of your name; upstairs, downstairs and out the front and back, up and down the street. When no response is heard, everyone in the house stops what they're doing, and strict orders are issued, don't no one come back into this house, until someone finds your little sister or brother.

My mom and dad knew back then, that the streets didn't give back. Once they claim something or someone, they made it their own. Blessed and beyond anyone else's belief, my parents would always find a way to snatch back what is theirs, no matter the circumstances.

Then you can best believe that you were going to get the belt or switches, and the repeated words," how many times have I told you?" While being restrained by the arms or held between their legs with repetitious whippings.

I am glad to say that my parents didn't raise any drug dealers, thugs, prostitutes, or thieves. They both made a vow to take you out first, before anyone or the streets ever got a chance. So, if you know what's best for you, you'd keep your little butt in the chair in the living room, or outside where everyone can see you or let someone know when you are going to play down the street or next door.

I DIDN'T KNOW

I didn't know what was wrong with me before I came to the doctor's office and I won't know until a later date. The receptionist informed that the Doctor will not be able to see me today. We will send him a message, and try to set up something for next week. I have never been in the habit of visiting the Doctor.

So, unless this thing carries over the next few days, I will probably forget why I even came here today. The last time was about five years ago, the time before that was about six years previously. I expect all the family pictures on his desk of his little, to be little adults on their way to College. And his stories and perspective of life would have greatly change.

But this will have to come on another day when he's not so busy and I am extremely sick, but I am glad I remembered when his office is, and they updated my files. Wish me well.

BACK ON THE BLOCK

I LOVE YOU MORE

I love you
more than
you will ever know.
I thought love
was something
you found,
and after
it got old
like a pair of sneakers,
you throw them away.
often looking back
and reminiscing about
the good times we shared
and those insatiable kisses
but the minute it looks
like things were falling apart
I figured it was time to move on
to someone new
one day I found myself alone
and I thought about you
by that time I come to the realization
that everyone and everything
gets old
you have to find a way
every day to make it new.
If you don't mind getting old
and gaining appreciative value,
do what you because no matter what,
I love you.

I AM SITTING

I am sitting in the doctor's reception area. They don't take a walk-ins, same-day appointments, or tolerate people that explain what their illness is. I want to see my doctor if sees me or I see him on the other side of the counter or glass panel door. He'll recognize me and the sense that I need to be seen.

I am willing to wait, and I don't want to have to come back in a few days. The receptionist utters out an appointment date, two weeks, I would be dead by then. "But sir if it's an emergency, we can have an ambulance an here in 5 minutes.."

I don't get it, but I do understand. I will sit back down, and wait it out until he's available to see me. I don't know what's wrong with me. I have a slight cold, a slight headache, and I slightly feel weak all over my body, esp. my legs. I feel like I just want to go running until I feel, whatever is in me, had gone away.

EXERCISE DAILY

In very few words, exercise daily like your life depended upon it.

Worship today, like there's no tomorrow.

Save a little each day, but you never know when you are going to need it.

Learn to love because it takes a lifetime to get it right.

May God bless you on your incredible journey.

IT'S SAD TO THINK

It's sad to think that most of you don't know what love is. You think it's when someone special holds your hands or kisses your lip. And this same person whispers in your ear how much they care about you, how they feel about you will last a million lifetimes.

 If you're thinking love is that person who said I do, and still laying there beside you, I have a little bad for you. Love is finding yourself alone, talking and walking with the only true unbegotten God.

When you can feel His holy presence. And when speaks you so softly like no other, then you realize true love. Everyone and everything is superficial or artificial to the real thing.

HUSH

Hush, where is your innocence? How did you feel, and what were you thinking when you're innocence left your body, mind, and spirit. Where is your innocence? Can you put your finger on it.

You're still innocent. No matter what has been taken from you, I am sure you still have some of your innocence left. But, the world doesn't have to know. That's up to you when you want to open of those doors and to whom ever you choose to share.

Hush, you are still innocent. Because you don't know everything, and everything has not been taken from you. That's the truth.

IT'S NOT WHAT YOU THINK

It's not what you think
It's not what you say.
For me, it's not really
about you.
Even though, you're
the first one to jump.
Every time I move
or have something to say,
I want to live my life
to the fullest;
a lily has its season;
it shares in the joys and pains
of others, but still reaches
it's potential before the end of its
lifetime.
I still have places to go
people to see, and as cliché as
it may sound
I have mountains
I must climb.
So, this isn't about you,
it's about me.
The only part of this
that becomes about you
is when I look up
and see you standing
in my way.

I AM HOPE

I am hope, when people see me running, that one day they will do the same, staying focus on the road ahead.

No matter the heat, snow, or rain I am hope, that when people ask I say to them this road never ends I only know my first step outside my door is where it begins.

As I was growing up to the corner then to school, and then to my grandmother's house, and back home.

I am hope. It clears the mind and renews your spirit. I have found that running gives you strength, determination, and allows you to stride towards the finish; long before most have decided to give up or quit, I am hope.

I OPENED MY EYES

I open my eyes and I realized. No pirates have taken over my ship and I looked out of the window my car is still parked where I left it.

As I was laying, lying I will never get published based on grammar I was trying to recall the dream I was having which had almost vanished from my memory, like walking out of a movie theater.

The scene of my dream had taken place on a small boat, with at least three cabins. I am just the narrator of the story. I sat back and watched the entire time.
There were about six guys on this boat, but three main characters. This when I became aware that I watching these guys that had just taken this young boy hostage.

I can overhear them discussing his worth. When his parents discover that he is missing, they are going to be willing to pay anything.

BACK ON THE BLOCK

PART OF ME

This is the part of me that you do not know when I play the love strings on my guitar. I am doing everything to walk away when everything inside of me is telling me no.

I don't want to be your loving man, I don't want to be a part of a big band. There's so much about me that you don't know. I am trying my best to walk away from you, while everything inside of me is telling me no. I am sitting here playing all the love strings on my guitar. If you don't leave now, it will be hard for me to let you go.

I have been in love before and I have been played a fool, so it's not so easy anymore for me to lose my cool. I am playing this love song that I feel way deep down in my soul.

I want you to stay, but I am begging you to go. There's so much more about me that you just don't know. Let me just keep on playing this song of love, until you walk out the door. I can't have just a little taste of you, without coming back, time after time for more.

LOVE HAS A WAY

Love has a way of finding you just when you least expect if you don't have look for love though it feels like a lifetime away. Because when love finally arrives, you are so caught off guard, you don't know what to say. Be patient, love is on its way its flight plans are your destination, just be ready to be caught off guard by someone with open arms.

Too many times we've given up and thrown in the towel, but when love arrives, the days and nights you spent worrying and wondering, will be more worth the while. Love has a face of an Angel, nothing but all smiles. So, you just have to wait for your love to arrive, and catch you by surprise.

THROUGH ALL THESE YEARS

I went through all these years and just realize I can't live without you when you went your way and I went mines I never hurt before now I have places in my heart that won't heal I started having difficulty breathing and finding the words to say. I know might be able to feel me on this. It took me this to realize the realness.

You made me happy and I didn't share that enough with you. I know can't turn back the hands of time, give you enough make up roses, but this love felt the appreciation of what was, is well overdue. I wasn't trying to look back, hold onto the past sometimes, you just have to find clarity before you can move on to someone new.

I GREW UP IN D.C.

I grew up in Washington D.C., I had to tell my son, "When you snob people, you're robbing people of who they are." I learned while growing up, clothes, shoes, jewelry, cars, and houses don't make the person.

If they don't have what it takes to treat people with dignity and respect, they are just as broke, poor, and deprived as a man with nothing on the streets. And be careful because a lot of them locked up, living below zero, and begging has all of us wrapped up into one.

It's a strange world son, but remember you might be looking in, looking up, or trying to get someone's attention. I remember what my mom always taught me, "Son, you always put people first, ahead of things." Things don't get you into heaven, people do.

BACK ON THE BLOCK

RIDING THE METRO

I am riding on the Metro bus. For some that might be an everyday occurrence but for me it's strange event. I had to walk a block past my street and decide for a minute which side I should stand on. I figured it out, as I was allowing the V-12 to get pass me.

I did ask someone who utilizes the Metro services, how much does it cost? I was like damn! Okay, I am at the Addison Metro, and before I got off the bus I asked the Driver for a transfer. She looked at me and explain, "Sir, you have to pay $1.70 each time you get on the Metro bus". And I said, damn again.

I didn't bring that much loose change with me. So, after asking a few more people, I am headed in the right direction, and I won't end in Atlantic City. The C-21 or C-22, I will wait for you. All the other Metro Bus won't get a chance to try my patience or work my nerve. Pardon me while I glance up at all the other potential riders. Mostly everyone seems content with holding their standing position.

A few, like myself, are listening to music streaming into their ear or chatting with someone on a cell phone. Dark color clothing, light jacket, knit or baseball cap seems to be the thing. I am wearing my burning orange running jacket, Dri-lock and wind resistance in case this bus doesn't show up.

Its here and folks are filing out and boarding like we were in some third world country, and someone is going to miss an opportunity for this luxurious ride. I am sitting down, but the guy beside me is sharing a portion of my seat as well. Dare I ask him, "Sir, can you scoot over". I am sure it would be difficult since he's hugging up the window seat.

I AIN'T GOT TO TELL YOU NOTHING'

I ain't got to tell you nothing'
you can ask all you want
I have rights, likes everyone else
I might look dumb,
but I'm not stupid.
We can sit here all night
but I am nothing talking...
until my lawyer come
I know that if I don't have one,
one will be appointed to me.
--Three hours later
I told yawl before
I ain't about to open my mouth
and confess to a crime I did not commit.
I was home all day yesterday watching T.V..
The only time I left the house was when I went
out for some milk for some cereal because we
were all out.
-- What time was that?
Man, I am not about to start yawl anything,
next yawl will have me on some trumped up
charges and locked up, like my friend Ray, Ray
for life.

NO DAY WAS EVERY PROMISED

No day was ever promised, only one breath was given. Everybody will try to tell you differently, put yourself in God's hands, or destiny plans to wipe you out. It's not a game of Jeopardy, Wheel of fortune or Let's Make A Deal with Monty Hall as your Host.

If you are going to live this life and onto the next, you are going to have learned to talk the talk, walk the walk in the name of the Father, Son, and Holy Ghost. It's past joke time, and someone else wiping and spanking your butt, if you really want to make it in this world, give the man upstairs your undivided attention. Read His word daily, and visit His house.

Don't take what I say or anyone else says as the gospel, with both hands in the air, go in surrendering, "Lord I am yours." It took me a long while, but its never too late, so long as you still have that first breath that He gave you, and say to Him, "Lord I want to be saved?" The choice is yours, its always been yours, salvation is free. Put your life in God's hands and live eternally, don't live your life to be a slave to the grave.

ONE OF THE HARDEST JOBS

One of the hardest jobs in the world is teaching everyone else's child to read and write. First, you have to teach them to keep their hands to themselves and not fight.

As they grow older it becomes increasingly difficult to hold their attention. They become less mindful of learning and restless

so you have to send them out of the classroom, because of their erratic behavior, and often sent home for suspension.

Teaching our children, your child; what are you doing as a parent or primary Care Taker to help make a difference? Before anyone figure points, make sure we are working as a team, so that your child, our children, are not ending up in jail, selling drugs, living below poverty, or just cannot compete, because they did not get all our or your attention and guided support.

BACK ON THE BLOCK

---Just tell us what time us

around time did you leave the house? Six hours later

Man, where is my lawyer? I am tired, hungry and my family is wondering what is happening to me. This is some bull, and you know it. Every Black man in America is not a criminal. I have been a law biting citizen all my life, whatever that means, but it sounds appropriate for this situation. Can I have my one phone call?

---As soon as you tell us, what store went to get the milk.

Are you serious, man I went to Arthur's Market right up to the street from me, before the Nationalize football game at 1 o'clock, and was back before kick off?

--- You have the right to remain silent; whatever you say will be used against you. You have the right to a Lawyer....

WTF did I do? WTF did I say?

WTF is going on? It is too got damn early in the morning for this.

All I know, this is some bull.

-- Mr. Brown your lawyer is here.

Lawyer-- I hope you were able to refrain from making a statement.

I HIT THE BOILING POINT

Yesterday, I hit that boiling point and yes I almost blew a gasket. I didn't see it coming at first but I must have been running hot all day.

I should have pulled off on the side of the road to cool off or at least to pray. But I kept pushing, until boy I was smoking.

That's when I felt my heart and looked at my temperature gauge, now I am here stuck in traffic and my face is filled with rage.

I should have, could have done a lot of things differently before it got to this point, I hope to take and learn from this experience that God will anoint.

BACK ON THE BLOCK

I SHOULDN'T TELL YOU

My worst fears
Being held captive
In the belly of a slave ship
Falling and falling
And not able to wake up
Seeing this vision that I have been having since I was a small child, a shadow of a man staring out of a nine-pane glass window.
I just want to shoot them, so the reality of it goes away another was when my son was small...
He went chasing after his red ball and he would not answer me when I call his name and. Not being able to get to him with my quickness
When an oncoming car was rapidly approaching and he and this little red ball was only feets from streets
And me at that time
Did not have a relationship with god or enough faith to stop and call on God
I am in such a better place now
And much of the fear in me is gone
It's a step-by-step process
But I am getting there,
One fear at a time.

I NEED YOU

I need you,
you are a habit
I can't quit.
I wake up paranoid
looking for you
like someone stole
all my shyt...
I love you,
that's the truth.
You are benefit
of my youth,
by any other name
you are my sunshine
I am helpless without you,
But hopefully we will be to-
gether.
I went to sleep last night
and woke up this morning
with your lips touching mine.
Sometimes a dream
lasts a lifetime.
I stop looking in the mirror
cause I don't like what I see
someone who is as fragile as
me.
I don't want to stand alone
my world has been built
around you, making me
strong.
you know you can save me
from self-destruction;
never leave me without a love
note and a set of instructions
baby you will be okay
but you know I can't stay.
Kind words, but still not
enough.

DON'T LOOK AT MY CLOTHES

Don't look at my clothes. Look at where God has bought me. Don't look at where I live. Look at where God has bought me. Don't look at what I drive or not driving. Look where God has bought me.
Don't look at things in life I lost and gain.
Look where God has bought me.
A man looks on the outside. But looks on the inside. I am far better off now, than I was before.
I had some growing up and going through to do. It was not pleasant. As I shook my head, and stomp my feet. A many day and night and I said to God, this does not feel good, or seem right. But I held on inside God's perfect little storm.

IN THE WORLD

In the world with so many people, no one touches me anymore not my heart, my soul or my pillow at night, I almost feel invisible to those I care about, as they sit beside me watching a 60" HD TV or on a private phone call like I was out of sight. Maybe I do need to grab the car keys and go out for a long drive think about making some changes in my life, so I can feel that I am alive.

I am not looking for a lot of attention I just don't want to be a part of someone else life, so when people see us together, they look at you all surprised like I was something or someone you failed to mention I feel that the person in my life is suspect, someone that you are so not so sure of, or possibly cannot trust.

As I am driving away from the house, the relationship and the person I thought I cared about, who has brought me to point, my grandmother's voice is in my ear, "there are too many windows and doors in a house, to stay inside something that's not working for you."

And she ain't never lied. I can't speak for anyone else, you have to make decisions for yourself, but know this, you are not a doormat, someone dishwasher, or butt kisser, and if you going to stay in some mess like that, don't complain so much, fix yourself up and show some pride.

Sometimes

Sometimes while you are walking, and not thinking about anything, you look down, not being really sure at first, but to your surprise it's money, lot of times it doesn't really matter the amount, it's the celebrated moment of someone else's loss and my gain.

I often ask myself, is this the game of life and how is it played? you work hard to keep the love you've earned and without paying attention, it' somehow fell away from you or left unattended, you go back looking for the love you've lost and some fool is jumping up and down screaming, finder's keepers!

FOR THOSE
THAT DON'T ME

For those that don't know me. I am a lion kept in his cage. I am an inmate to the words on this page. My silence is held captive by my rage.

I can't keep this pretense. I don't like what they've made me a fighter to the finish, even if someone tastes me.

You just don't lie there unless your conscientious man is totally unaware defeat only comes when I can't get up, left to dogs or six feet under and covered up.

I REMEMBER

I remember Pops

Be a man

Be a father

To your son

Be a protector

Of your daughters

Be patient with each one

Be a husband

To your wife

Learn to love her

And treat her right

Be kind to yourself

Life will have you

Going in a lot of directions

Chose a path of your own

But most importantly son

Be happy.

YOU CAN'T

You can't go through this world and not know who your friends are. Haven't you wanted to know and not have to guess, who your ride or die you are?

The best people are so whack you always have to watch your back. I am one true to the code, I will do whatever it takes short of selling my soul.

If I can see you, I will get to you, and if I can hear you, I will bust through a brick wall if you decide to take a leap of faith. I will help break your fall.

I don't have second thoughts; there is never enough time. I always treat everything like a ticking bomb. I believe a best friend is someone that will always be there to rescue you no matter what, before your world blows up or you have nowhere else to turn.

I JUST WANT TO KNOW

I just wanted to know if they still love me? So I said "I love you" and I got no response, so I am thinking they didn't hear me.
So I got in front of their face and before I could repeat myself, they turned and walked away.
I was feeling good, but somehow it slowed my engine down as I went throughout my day.
It took me out the race and doesn't seem worth winning now. I tried to find the reason why and we've been around this tree before.
love is a question that many times cannot be answered just enjoy the ride, wear your helmet, and stop trying to keep score.

EVEN I STRUGGLE EACH DAY

Even I struggle each day to find the words to say that will help me defined the ways I feel about you. I want the words to come out of my mouth because its meaning will help me describe the depths of my soul and the things that go through mine, when I cannot maintain my control, whenever I realize there is no me, without you.

Visualize heaven with no stars. Internalize a baby being born with no eyes I didn't realize that I was so fragile hanging onto for dear life with every breath that you take away from me, when there are moments (I am sure) that you turn away (even walk) or not thinking of me. It's not a matter of being able to handle the truth.

I know the truth. I am glad that I found you or you found me, but unarguably we are bound (body, mind, and spirit) together. I love you Jesus and I am not ashamed to express this side of me to you or the world, for there is no other like you.

WHEN I DREAM IN COLOR

When I dream in color, this is for the person whose house is on fire. They feel trapped in a room with little ventilation the relation that you are in gives you little to live for but you don't want to jump out the window or throw your life.

Sometimes is so much better than what you and I can envision, and I am not to sit here and paint you a pretty picture. But if you get up and go to your window of pain, don't look down look up to god, with thanks and praise. Then and there you find your fire escape ladder waiting for you to get out of a burning house.

Don't ever think that you are not loved or no one can love you. God will take you at his doorstep or where ever you are right now. Don't deny yourself, real love. Amen

IN THE GAME OF CHESS

In the game of chess and in life the king always protect his queen and never leaves her out in the open. A lot of us make a bad move, which amounts to dumb decisions

You just have to ask yourself, how important is the woman in your life, mother of your children (because nobody just has one) and who has gone out their way to help you maintain your reign.

She's not sacrificial, she's beneficial, and without her it would be difficult to win the game. I know, you want to show her who's boss, who wears the pants, but the reality is about being partners, not having power struggles or ego trips. Survival is based on what we can do for each other, not destroy each other. Because, men without our queen, game over.

MY DAD WAS ALWAYS THERE

My dad was always there from the moment I open my eyes, until the day Lord closed his. I can only characterize him in a fairytale manner because he was unbelievable. Ideas, thoughts and things were always happening in his heads. It was like someone or angels were always telling him something.

Because whenever you tried to interrupt him during a thought being processed, he'd hold up his index finger, signaling you to give him a minute. And out of that time span. He would have the equation to solve the problem, be able to describe and formulate into words, what it would take most people with doctorate degree to figure out, let alone explain.

 He could always take what little he had, share almost others and make the most it. He was a lion in the jungle, a bear that protected his family and friend, Counselor in the courtroom, an Architect of an idea, but most importantly, he most would never run off give up, he was my dad.

I THOUGHT I BURNED THIS BRIDGE

I thought I burned this bridge. I watched it burn; I got choked in its smoke, and then I ran off like a little punk ass as I got burnt by a little piece of cinder.

I didn't know how to tell you goodbye, I figured you'd keep pressing the issue, like now and you wouldn't leave me alone. Why can't you be a man about you? Confront me when there's a problem. I hate when men just run off to the next city, town or woman.

Just say, the same damn things in my ears with your pants up that you were saying when your pants were down, Baby we can do this all night long. What happened?

You got in a relationship and started having motion sickness, and decided to up and leave without notifying, with the quickness. As my girl Mary J. Blige would say, I should have left your ass a long time ago, and I'm not going to love no more. I wanted to let you know, I hope this child that I am carrying doesn't grow up to be anything like you.

BACK ON THE BLOCK

AT THE END OF MY LIFE STORY

At the end of my life's' story. I want to look up from my coffin and say to my Lord, "I am ready to come home. I helped raise my children and made sure they properly fed before they went to bed. I watch them from the front door or window, as they went to school and came home each day."

I made have failed on occasion but I listened to what they had to say. I allowed them to listen while I prayed. I encouraged them each day, eat well, play hard, and don't get caught in all the mess outside this door, stay close to home, and I want to see you when the street lights come on. I had enough time to appreciate my parents for the work they started in me, not knowing how I was going to turn out, I couldn't give them any guarantees.

Now, I can say it's time for me to give back, especially for all the years you two carried me. I have no regrets; I took in enough Sunday school classes, to never forget. God is love and you, your son and the spirit that you put in me, are the coolest trio, I thank you this opportunity, so I will be ready when its time for me to go.

I WANT TO GO STRAIGHT

I want to go straight, play it straight; it feels like the first time all over again. I am sure some of you can relate. Taking something that doesn't belong to you, and then start having second thoughts of taking it back. I know our momma' taught us better, and we know everyone that's out there, is not doing it to buy crack.

I like the feel of money in my pockets, a tight roll of 20's and 50's in a knot, and I would peel a twenty in front of people, so they see what I am about. I didn't want to go through life with people looking at me funny like I can't afford to live next door to them and be to dress my children up, and not feel like the police are coming after me, every time I am out running.

I had to pick and decide its time for a change before I find myself doing time for some stupid stuff. I would rather walk around with grumbled up newspaper coming out of sneakers. And live in a cardboard box, then throw my life away and end up being locked up. I would rather take my chances going without the luxuries and a few amenities, that's where I am at, that's just me.

BACK ON THE BLOCK

I STILL LOOK AROUND FOR YOU

I still look around for you, and I can't believe you're gone. We grew up walking to school, pushing over trash cans, and taking hits back and forth before the first-morning bell. I was nice, but you'd turn around and go back home.

I still look for you, we used to hang on the corner, in the shadow of the night, talking about how when we grow up, we're going to do something with our lives, while getting high.

After a few days, I come over for a visit and you come to the door, and say, "This is not a really good time." Many years have gone by, and I still look for you, but I think you have gone to a whole new high, without a chance to pack your bags or say goodbye.

I TOOK YOU FOR GRANTED

I took you for granted,
I should have been throwing
rose petals at your feet.
I didn't think I'd be here wondering
the next chance we'd meet.
When I was with you,
I should have made every moment last forever.
Boy, was I surprised
when I thought you were mine.

But I learned I wasn't that smart or clever.
Everyone loses at love sometimes,
but that's the only time I was caught off guard.
And I was blind.
I still hurt deep.
Through you, I will never see it in your face or hear
it in a sidebar conversation.
I think maybe only in my sleep
love came and left
without warning.
No time to prepare...
And leaving me in ruin...
and my life in despair.

WE THRIVE

We thrive
Despite the pain, we feel.
We strive,
despite the world, we live in
We realize, God comes
before everything.

Despite what people say or do to us.
we have to move forward
We baptize (in the name of Jesus).
Despite what the enemy tries to do to us,
Gods kingdom and His love are forever.

We agonize,
despite all, we know about Him,
we still lose faith at times and turn away from
Him
We idolize,
Yet despite all these things,
God loves us unconditionally.

TIME SERVED

You will never ever get me on some dumb stuff.
I've watched too many people I know go down.
Locked up behind bars, where they can't see the sky or the stars.
I went for a visit and I could see how they've hardened up, but still, they couldn't hide their inside tears.
I'm doing everything I know that is right, I don't even pretend to be a thug or have any acquaintances with a drugs.
I have and will punk out every time to avoid a fight.
I know barbells and dumbbells will make you stronger.
I don't want to see the insides of any prison, and I don't want the insides to know me.
There's not enough of time to throw hopes and dreams away for any man.

I WANT YOU TO BE STRONG

I want you to be strong. Keep believing in God for the little things. I know I say and think some crazy things in my head, especially when it comes to God....I know how to pray, but when I talk to God, I talk to Him, the way I'm talking to you now....." Lord, you know what I stand in need of, even before I ask... You knew me before I was born ... I am not complaining Lord, I just... want to know the reason for my storm....I remember when I was younger in Christ and I gave my life to you, I said, have your way oh Lord.... Nothing will ever stand between me and you...That hasn't changed.... Here I am again Lord, before your throne in mercy.... I need you to heal the body and spirit of those that need you, Lord....I am your weeping child, these tears of mines flow.... I am not ashamed to cry or pray Lord.... I love my friends and family, and I humbly ask you to touch the hearts of my enemies. ....Thank you, Lord, for all you've done and going to do, in Jesus name, Amen."

NEIGHBOR'S LOVE R STREET

Flowers in the Spring don't grow everywhere. I grew up in a neighborhood that everything didn't look so pretty, but the people were beautiful.

Mr. and Ms. Robertson, Mr. and Mrs. Davis on each side of us. The Clarks, and Norris; I can't leave out Washington's, Gerald's and Thomas, along with the people across the street; up and down the street. I could go on forever naming my neighbors and their children, but we were more than neighbors. This city block was family.

I often look back and wonder where did everyone go? But I know. Many moved away, some got caught -up by the snares in life, and a few were called home by God, along with those few before their time, with the shame of crime.

They've moved on to greener sceneries, just a handful remained behind. But all of them I still play with, talk to and think about in my mind. I miss those days and I loved them all. And, there's no prettier flower than a neighbor's love.

TWO KINDS OF PEOPLE

There are two kinds of people in the world, people that look cute and the ones that think they are cute.
These people that think they are cute, really aren't cute and we have to pray for them.
 The only real cute people are the ones that smile all the time, and they're crazy.
Seriously, you can see them walking up and down on my street.
Don't wave! That's what they do all day, smile and wave at everybody and everything. And, you're just as crazy as they are if you think you're cute.

YOU DON'T KNOW YOUR CHILD

You don't know your child, your child knows you. You can't beat your child like you use to but now that child is trying your patience, and wanting to beat you.

They came into this world looking at your ugly mug, staring you up and down from the front in their high chair or crib, then at the back of your shoulders, neck, and head; studying your every move.

By the time they hit their teens, they have profiled you and know how to counter-act your every move, acute no answer that's slicker Vaseline.

You want to choke them at times because now they are talking loud and trying to fight back. That's when you have to catch your wind or two; get back in the ring with them and double up on your punches, throw a hook and then an uppercut, then let them know I brought you into the world, and I will have no problem take you out.

There are still some things you haven't seen, and mama hasn't shown you. Keep messing up and you won't make it to your next birthday. Now, go clean up your damn room like I told you! Before I mop this floor up with you. This is what ugly really looks like.

PEOPLE CAN BE MEAN

I did not know that people could be so mean and that there are so many other mean, rude, nasty and obnoxious people feeling the same way towards other people, for one reason or another, making this a mean world.

I didn't know either that there are so many mean people living and working in such close proximity of me. And just because they like me, and dislike the person beside me, don't change the way I feel about them. They are still a mean person for disliking a person based on their personal prejudices.

It makes it hard for me to be like them. I feel something in my heart against those that don't treat everyone else the same, regardless of their differences. And accept others for who they are and where they are.

God made us all different, but also in His image. We can not be mean to God by disliking people that do not look or act like us. As my mother would say, "Let's not act ugly."

We need to treat all God's people with respect and serve notice to ourselves about prejudices, racism and discrimination. Bottom line, stop being mean to each other because God does not like ugly.

YOU'RE NOT ALONE

You're not alone, nor the only one that gets up out of bed, look out the window of proposedly of hopes and dreams. I am saddened on those days that I don't feel or see nothing. My bed is close to the window, I get back in it. I lay on my side away from the window, and I try not to think about it.

But, a thought comes to my head, "I must have missed something." I roll out of bed, put on my running shoes, snatch my iPod off the nightstand, and grab my jacket off the hook by the front door.

Now, I'm on the track stretching, taking deep breaths, and about to give this track a whipping; sorry I think my parents were a little abusive; I remember too many of my spankings. And, I didn't think the crime fit the punishment.

But, when I get out here running, its here I have a chance to clear my head, and think about not repeat that pattern. Sometimes, you don't know what's happening in your life, when you're in it.

So, I realize I have to jump up and leave out the house, run if I have to, to get a better perspective. Looking out your window, or going back to bed is not always going to do it.

CIVIL DISOBEDIENCE

Whenever I was told to do something as a child. It was like I didn't hear a word either one of my parents were saying to me.

Many times I had to hear my name being called before I was ignoring them bout their request went to a place in my head immediately, that could care less.

Timeless was this process of disobedience and countless whippings that followed. I never said no, that wasn't going to do it. Its just that I was busy playing, watching T.V. or preoccupied with my own thoughts.

I just know that disappointment and I were very close friends. Things that were important to you just were not important to me. Such as cleaning my room, taking the trash out, washing the dishes, mopping the floor and the list of chores that went beyond my expectations for job specification as a child. This was my play time.

They needed to hire someone, I should have been paid for indentured services. I know it doesn't work like that but that's how a child thinks.

I DON'T OWE YOU SHYT

Have you ever had someone say to you, "You owe me?" And your proper response should have been, "I don't owe you shyt!"

Don't think for one moment because you were there with baiting breath to help my cause in my hour of need, that I am supposed to reduce my level of social standards, so you can seduce me to your ignorance.

For your payment in full I told you, "Thank you" and in case you missed it, "God bless you."

I don't like people like that. See you falling, help you up and want something for their troubles.

"Girl got to fight falling down and standing up, 'cause these suckers will try to get you like vultures if they think you don't have any more fight left in you."

GETTING HIGH

Getting high never solved any real world problems. Getting drunk takes time off your clock.
Being functional without recreational substances is the best way to live your life, and avoid unprotected sex and those who don't protect themselves.

Learn to love yourself and trust your instincts, especially when it's time to walk away. You came into the world alone, you don't owe anyone anything. You owe it to yourself to be happy, and not to have to find happiness.

A REAL FRIEND

Sometimes it takes a person longer then what they expect to grow up. Often, leaving friends and family to move on without them.

This is not a situation where you feel guilty about leaving simple people to act out alone. We know eventually they'll come around, but it's something they have to do on their own because at the expense others are costly.

For a long time, I was lost and I didn't do or say the things that would keep people from distancing themselves from me. I am good now. I've learned to put things into perspective and focus on the positives in life.

I admit only to myself, I don't have it all figured out, but nothing keeps me from thanking the man upstairs, He never gave up on me when everyone else had disappeared.

So, I pray God always allow me to be the best friend I can be, and stay beside that person in spite of themselves or what they may be going through.

BACK ON THE BLOCK

LONG WAY FROM HOME

Yes, I am a long way from home. And the time away has slipped away from me. As I sit back I can see and remember everyone back on the block; some doing good, a few shooting bad but each in their mind trying to figure it out.

That's why I moved away from the area. I was trying to figure it all out. Where did God want me to be? The noise in my family's house was too loud, and I couldn't hear myself think or concentrate on anything of importance.

There was always too much of people running and guns popping to be hanging out on the streets, especially in my youth. I needed to be somewhere else other than here. And before I could make my own decision, the decision was already made for me. I was paid a visit by a United States Marines Recruiter. He laid out the perfect plans for my future, leaving out a few non evasive steps in the process, but I survive. I have many stories to tell, but this one was about how I got away.

I march to a different drum beat. I have my opinion but I am not opinionated. I do pass judgment, by my judgment is based on morals and ethics that I had been taught and raised on. I don't have to remind myself that we're all different, and our differences are not all visible. But, if we can all learn to love and respect one another differences, we wouldn't be fighting abroad or inside our borders.

 So, our families and neighbors, and the day to day threat of our way of life can be safe for everyone. I try my best to always go to God first, to see where He needs you and me to be through prayer.

KEEP BELIEVING

Friend, I want you to be strong. Keep believing in God for the little things. I know I say and think some crazy things in my head, especially when it comes to God....I know how to pray, but when I talk to God, I talk to Him, the way I'm talking to you now..." Lord, you know what I stand in need of, even before I ask... You knew me before I was born... I am not complaining Lord, I just want to know the reason for my storm... I remember when I was younger in Christ and I gave my life to you. I said, have your way Oh Lord... Nothing will ever stand between you and me...That hasn't changed ... Here I am again Lord, before your throne in mercy... I need you to heal the body and spirit of those that need you, Lord... I am your weeping child, these tears of mines flow from the rive of Jordan... I am not ashamed to cry or pray Lord... I love my friends and family, and I humbly ask you to touch the hearts of my enemies as well... Thank you, Lord, for all you've done and going to do, in the precious name of Jesus, Amen.

1st And R STREET

You told me, you went back to the old neighborhood. In my mind, I never left. I still keep the beat of the streets in my heart and soul. Whenever I go into battle, I don't feel like I am by myself, I swing high, kick low, and come at them with something they are not expecting. Even when you are against more than one, you have to let them know where you come from.

We never back down, despite the odds. The streets teach you, you have to go hard. This doesn't mean you will win every fight. It only means you gave them something to think about. You can't go through life letting people treat you any kind of way or they will think you are a punk.

If you forget where you came from and the things you went through growing up, maybe you need to go back. In my heart and my mind I never left, "So watch yourself."

AWAKENED

I was awakened by the Spirit that God has put inside of me. I got up with a purpose and that's to work to obtain steps through life that will allow me to give thanks and praise to Him continuously.

I know some days will be difficult, and many of them will be because I have drifted away or my fault. But I know in my heart, the Lord is my Sheperd, and I shall not want. And He will keep me if I ask Him to.

There are times I am really beside myself and I don't ask, and I find myself alone and in an awful way. But we all have to try to get up with the Spirit that God has put into us and live each day the best way we can.

Photo Shoot

I thought this morning run was going to be a photoshoot, with lights, cameras, action. As I stretched my legs and arms and warmed up for what I thought was going to be a dry run, I took exceptional notice to one of the adversaries warming up and stretching in the same like fashion.
I should have known something was up when I arrived and the parking lot wasn't empty. Filled with spectators. As I got out of my vehicle; someone yelled out, "What are you going to do for the first two miles?"
 It's my practice to never let the opposition know what I'm about to do. I shook off the cold, and I convinced myself not to beat myself by starting off too fast. And whatever you do, don't look behind you.
I never saw this coming, and it was too late to change my stride. Now, I had to make up the distance I had lost between us. Just think we were once Lovers and more than friends, and now we're sitting in the courtroom and letting them decide who's the winner.
And what about the children that belong to both of us? Go ahead, you are the winner. I will take my loses like a man. As a runner, I should have run when I had the chance.

IN YOUR EAR

I know you heard it in your ear, stay out off them streets. They will, if you not careful, mess you up for life. They come with a price tag that neither one of us can afford, my children.

If we are all sitting around watching a little T.V. for dinner, when suddenly discovered that one of us is missing.

A shout out is given in the house of your name, upstairs. downstairs and out the front and back, up and down the street. When no response is heard, everyone in the house stops what they're doing, and strict orders are issued, don't no one come back into this house, until someone finds your little sister or brother.

My mom and dad knew back then, that the streets didn't give back. Once they claim something or someone, they made it their own.

Blessed and beyond anyone else's belief, my parents would always find a way to snatch back what's is theirs, no matter the circumstances. restrained by the arms or held between their legs.

Then you can best believe that you were going to get the belt or switchs, and the repeated words, "How many times have I told you?" While being with repetitious whippings.

I am glad to say that my parents didn't raise any drug dealers, thugs, prostitutes, or thieves. They both made a vow to take you out first, before anyone or the streets ever got a chance. So, if you know what's best for you, you'd keep your little butt in the chair in the living room, outside where everyone can see you or let someone know when you are going to play down the street or next door.

IN A DARK PLACE

You are not the only one in this world that's living in a dark place. You tell everyone you don't have an address. It's not at you mind having the company but you also know that after 2-3 minutes they'd be looking to leave.
I know me, I'd be trying way too hard to convince them and myself that I am a normal person, but my issues would come rambling repeatedly out of my mouth. You know, we hate when this happens.
"Would you like to sit down? Would you like to sit down? Or if you want to stand that's perfectly okay too."
I seldom ever get any company, so I feel like a nervous wreck, sweating in cool places. " I really think you should leave now."

All of us need a little help, some of us way more than others. I am not usually a patron but I do like sitting in McDonald's from breakfast time to dinner in a corner, ear hustling until management asks me to leave.

I've learned I am not alone with my issues. It's just that some of y'all are able to hide it very well, to the point it doesn't seem too obvious and you don't stay patronize as long as I do.

The floor of the back of my closet is real. The courageous first step is admitting you have a closet and the problems you have are real. And most importantly that you need help. There I said it, I love listening to other people's problems at McDonald's. These people are nuts.

PICK A POINT

Pick a point,
any point, it's cold outside.
Don't play on the ice...
Don't play with real
guns or fake ones.
Sit up straight, play it straight,...
and no shooting real
guns or pointing them
at your sister or brother, body or face.
It's sad that no one has told you this.
Often a misfired gun doesn't miss.
It's too cold inside the jail cell;
trying to find or scrape
up enough change so
my son can make bail.
If I've said it once,
I've said it a million times:
Stay in school
Play by and follow the rules.
Listen to the Teacher
for oral and written instructions.
Don't do stupid stuff,
get caught doing dumb junk,
or else you'll spend or regret
most of your adult life saying,
what you should have, could have done, if I had only
listened to my parents or someone else along the way.

BACK ON THE BLOCK

Being where we are now, nothing else explains it better. So, I try a little harder each day. Trying to make up for the days, month and years, for the assignments in school, that I never turned in. No one, just me, to blame.
Pick a point, any point is the point. For a positive purpose life. The thing about time is that it never stops, but unfortunately, we're only afforded opportunities within a short span of it. By God's grace and mercy, we'll enjoy some of it, before we kick the bucket.

R Street

A VISIT FROM DAD

I remember this one particular time while growing up, my father had asked me to do something, and it was to go out and buy him a pack of cigarettes at night, from a store further from the house than I'd usually have to go because everything else was closed.

Before I took the money out of his hands, I'd look up at him and said, "Dad, I am scared to go all the way at this time of night by myself." He'd say, "You're not going by yourself, take one of your brothers that's asleep with you, just don't come back without my cigarettes." I'd say, Dad, one more time, before I knew I was crossing the imaginary line of him losing his post dramatic stressed mind; there's a lot of scary people out there that might try to approach us.

He'd then say, "Come a little closer to me, look me in the eyes son. The only person you have to be afraid of is me. Now, before I get upset, you and one of your brothers go out there and bring me back a pack of Kool cigarettes."

BACK ON THE BLOCK

My father didn't play, when he told you to do something, he meant it. Failure in understanding his verbal orders would more than likely result in a butt whipping. His lasting effect, still kind of bothers me, especially when I remind my children that they really don't know how good they got it.

And you were right again dad, I have never been more afraid of anything or anyone, other than not going out at night as a child, and bringing you back a pack of cigarettes. Not ever have I said, "When I'm not there, I'm there." I mean I'm there in other ways, not in the physical sense.

But, I am still there. You don't see me, and you don't have to see me, just know that I am there, if you need me. I know it doesn't make sense, it doesn't have to make sense, just know that I love you, and that's all that matters.

STUNG TWICE

I'm not too afraid to admit it; I was stung twice... I want you to listen carefully... These streets ain't nothin' to play with ...regardless of how much you think you know, you don't know shyt... Everybody out here thinks they're smarter and can outsmart the next man....because they always think they have a better plan, to hit you with something unexpected...Yeah your boys and everyone else around you, make you believe that you're the badest, coolest and rudest thug...Because you've always gotten away from a scene without getting caught....knocked mugs out every time you fought...

You have people believing that being a hood with your pants sagging down is all good.....Now you're buying and selling drugs on both sides of town...Rolling in the dough, and everybody's calling you the playboy of Southside; Gradually but eventually you've forgotten everything you were ever taught....grandma said," Be careful baby, them streets are dangerous; stay out there too long, you'll eventually get hurt," came to your head... And at this moment, God saw fit for you to live...These dreams I be having...God be getting my attention...You can die here...or live to tell others. Ain't God good!

BACK ON THE BLOCK

Second chances later, you're looking up because you can't get up, your mind is riddled by a bullet in your chest, and your blood is spilling like liquor all over the place....you can see your hands and legs but they won't move.....It's God that you want to talk to now, but some young punk with a .22 caliber is standing over you, taking your jacket and shoes, saying," I expected more of a fight, you ain't cool." Lying in your own pool of blood, in a dead man's alley, every conceivable thought of where you went wrong, and how you really disappointed your grandmother now.

I DON'T HAVE TIME

I don't have time, don't want to do time. So, you won't see me scraping seeds across the table. Don't feel like trippin, dippin or ill'n when I am able to stand up on my own two feet without slippin'. I like spitt'n and free-stylin' about life.

I am all about grinding. Not sell'n out, snitch'n in the kitchen, with a crew that don't do anything but bitch'n. You can hate on me but you'd be wasting your time because I won't converse with you or rehearse with you, I won't even acknowledge you in my next rhyme.

Cliché', life is too short, holler at me while I take my game to the court. I promise to pay my baby's mama because I don't need all the drama so the Judge gave me another chance to play catch up on Child Support.

I don't blame her because all the children in the world have to eat, wear decent clothes and have someone there for them when or if they think, and assure them it's not their fault.
I, we have to do better for the generations coming afterward. Or world war iii will be our children fighting against their fathers and mothers. This is where we are now.

My Momma

I know the only reason that I'm in the world and here today is because of my momma. My momma brought me into this world, and for her, at the time it was a struggle. I know she didn't have all the love and support she needed, but my momma was always there for me.

So, when things in life seemed to be so tough, I always think about my momma, and the things she would say to me, Son, some days are going to be hard, and it's going to feel like it's just you against the world.

But that's not the time you turn away and cry, or ball-up your fist because you're mad. I would hope that you pray to God, for strength and understanding to withstand until another day."

To me, my momma means everything. I hope a day does not go by, that I don't think about her or tell other people about my momma. Because without my momma, where would I be?

I love you momma, and I thank you for being the tree rooted by the river of life, and forever sharing your knowledge and wisdom with me, and those around you.

When I prayed

Last night, while I knelt down and prayed, I ask God why aren't my prayers for the people that I love, saving them from sickness, being locked-up, or from going down a crooked path in life?

He said in a whisper, I almost didn't think my prayers would save you, but I never stopped believing in you.

People make their own choices in life, and as much as you and I want the best for them, they have to want it for themselves.

After God finished speaking, it didn't keep the tears from rolling down even more, but I stayed down on my knees praying for them, hoping they want better for themselves, and for me to keep believing in Him and them through faith.

BACK ON THE BLOCK

What Are Brothers For?

What are brothers for? My mother and father always said, watch your brother, and make sure he doesn't hurt himself, and don't let them get into any trouble. Or I will hold you totally responsible.

After I grew up, I left home and went straight into the United States Marine Corps. Every day pretty much the same. They yelled and screamed, that we're brothers and a team. And nowhere else in the world will you find, "No man will be left behind."

To the depths of hell and up to the steps of heaven, I will come and get you, my brother. Without another word from those that have always been in my ears. With tears I am praying for my brother and that my prayers save him.

What I had to learn without confusion, is that if you want to successfully rescue someone or anyone, you have to go in and come away with Jesus as your covering.

Son

You are going to fail miserably in life, when you don't pay attention, follow instructions, or listen to sound advice. When you fall, and you will fall, the world will be looking and laughing as you bust your ass, and it won't be from slipping on a sheet of ice.

You don't have to get it every day like the Washington Post, but you damn well better know that you will be held accountable for your actions, especially when you're found guilty of doing the most.

I am not the Judge or Jury for any man's convictions, nor do I have a heaven or hell to put them in. I will only do what God has ordained me to do, and that's to preach and teach in His name.

Walk as I walk with me. Pray as I pray with me. Son, there will come a day when I will no longer be with you. My hopes are, and I quote, "In all you're getting, I pray that you get understanding."

This world can be a cold, desolate place, but to change this we have to first seek God in the dark places of our own heart and mind, and when you get there, let Him know that you need Him.

I would not be the man that I am today if I had not fallen a few times. And I wouldn't be the man that I am if I didn't share with you that it was Jesus who saved me.

And every day I wake-up I keep holding onto His hem. To all the brothers and sisters, sons and daughters, mothers, and fathers, I pray that when you fall, you fall away from your sin. Amen.

Poetry and Prose
Written by Ralph A. Watkins Jr

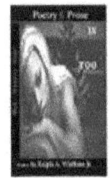

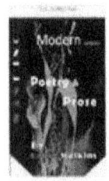

BACK ON THE BLOCK

www.ingramcontent.com/pod-product-compliance
Lightning Source LLC
Chambersburg PA
CBHW022117090426
42743CB00008B/894